Four Cheerful Chipmunks

Joan Thompson
Illustrations by Doug Roy

HAMPTON-BROWN

One bright day in sunny May,
four cheerful chipmunks plan a
picnic lunch.

One roasts a chicken.
One bakes muffins.
One picks cherries, and
one gets some cheese.
  "Yum, yum," they say. "What a
great lunch!"

Four cheerful chipmunks pack a picnic for the beach.

One packs the chicken.

One packs the muffins.

One packs the cherries, and one packs the cheese.

"Let's go!" they say.

Four cheerful chipmunks run down to the beach.

Out drops the chicken.

Out drop the muffins.

Out drop the cherries, and out drops the cheese.

Uh, oh! They don't know!

Four hungry foxes go home from
the beach.

One sees the chicken.

One sees the muffins.

One sees the cherries, and
one sees the cheese.

"What luck!" they say.

Four hungry foxes grab up all the lunch.

One grabs the chicken.

One grabs the muffins.

One grabs the cherries, and one grabs the cheese.

"Yippee!" they say. "Let's eat!"

7

Four cheerful chipmunks unpack their lunch.

"What happened to our chicken?"
"What happened to our muffins?"
"What happened to our cherries?"
"What happened to our cheese?"
"WHAT HAPPENED TO OUR LUNCH?" they cry. "Where did it go?"

Four not-so-cheerful chipmunks
spot four hungry foxes eating up
their lunch.

One is eating chicken.

One is eating muffins.

One is eating cherries, and
one is eating cheese!

"Hey!" cry the chipmunks. "Give
us back our lunch!"

Eight very angry animals tug on the lunch.

"It's mine!" yells a fox.

"No, it's mine!" yells a chipmunk.

"Give it here!" yells a fox.

"Give it back!" yells a chipmunk.

"Hand it over!" yells a fox.
"Give it up!" yells a chipmunk.
"Let go!" yells a fox.
"No, you let go!" yells a chipmunk.

"Stop it, you foxes! Stop it, you chipmunks. Stop it! Stop it! Stop it, please! Just stop right where you are and think how to end this fight," says Officer Tom.

13

Four angry chipmunks and four angry foxes think and think and think.

A fox says, "We found the lunch."

A chipmunk says, "We lost our lunch."

A fox says, "We want to keep it."

A chipmunk says, "We want it back."

A fox says, "We want to eat it."

A chipmunk says, "We all want to eat it!"

And then a chipmunk says, "Well,
why not? There is enough for all!"

Four cheerful chipmunks and four
happy foxes sit down to eat. All they
have to say is:

"Pass the chicken."

"Pass the muffins."

"Pass the cherries."

"Pass the cheese."

"Thank you, Fox."

"Thank you, Chipmunk."

"Please." "Please." "Please."